Horse Jokes

Funny Jokes for Horse Lovers

Aaron Stark

Horse Jokes

What's a horse's favorite dinosaur? *The broncosaurus.*

Why would a horse make a good president? *They know how to lead.*

What do ponies look for in a vehicle? *Lots of horsepower.*

How does a horse make paper mâché? *With newspaper clip-clop-pings.*

How do baby horses get tucked in at night? *They get told a tail.*

How does a rude princess sit on a horse? *Snide-saddle.*

What did the Clydesdale use to deal cards at the casino? *A horse-shoe.*

What does a horse call its treats? *My greatest preakness.*

Where do the cool horses live? *In rad-docks.*

How could you tell the horse gained weight? *It had extra girth.*

How do you wash a horse? *On a sponge-line.*

Why did the pony turn himself in? *He felt rem-horse.*

How did the horse get up the stairs? *He mounted them.*

Why was the horse such a good dancer? *It perfected its halturn.*

What's a horse's favorite dance move? *Watch me whip, now watch me neigh neigh.*

Why didn't the horse buy a house? *The costs were mounting.*

Why was the horse a great editor? *She was very thorough bred.*

How do horses show gratitude? *Flank you very much.*

Why don't horses like to parallel park? *They hate touching the curb.*

What does Pegasus like to do when he's bored? *Some dra-wing.*

What do you call a swimming donkey? *A silly seahorse.*

Why did the horse stop playing online games on her computer? *She had a high gallo-ping.*

Why did the horse get a pet bird? *It wanted more feathering.*

What's a horse's favorite way to style its mane? *In a ponytail.*

Why was the horse in charge? *It outflanked the others.*

What does a horse use to pin paper to her mood board? *Tack.*

What's a horse's least favorite fashion design? *Branding.*

Who did the ponies send out to retrieve a kidnapped package? *The task f-horse.*

Where do horses put their garbage? *In a land-filly.*

Where do horses sell their paintings? *At an art gallop-ry.*

What's a hippie horse's favorite music festival? *Stagecoachella.*

What are stuffed animal unicorns made of? *Pegaplush.*

What music festival do horses attend? *Lola Appaloosa.*

What did one horse say to its annoying sibling? *Canter you not?*

How do you tell a winged horse to be quiet in the library? *Pegashush.*

What's a horse's favorite accessory? *A purse.*

Why didn't the horse want to be named in the newspaper? *It wanted to remain a-pony-mous.*

What's a horse's favorite rapper? *Meg the Stallion.*

How does a horse do its hair? *With hunter clips.*

What did the winged horse move into its new house? *Its pegastuff.*

Why did the Arabian have such a temper? *It was hotblooded.*

What kind of computer does a horse want? *A Macintosh.*

Which horse is most into geography? *A fjord horse.*

What did the horse say when it tripped? *"Help, I've fallen and can't giddy-up."*

What does Pegasus have on Instagram? *A follo-wing.*

What's a horse's favorite classical musician? *Balk.*

Why was the horse so rude? *It kept instirrupting.*

What do horses put on pancakes? *Maple stirrup.*

How does a horse take a picture? *With the fish-hay lens.*

What's a racehorse's favorite meal? *Stakes.*

What horses are the best in school? *Grade horses.*

What kind of horse is best at art? *Paints.*

Why was the horse so quiet? *It was unsound.*

What's a horse's favorite type of dress? *A halter dress.*

How can you tell a unicorn is pregnant? *She'll be sho-wing.*

Why is Pegasus so good at switching leads? *He does flying lead changes.*

What's Maybelline's catchphrase for its horse clientele? *Maybe she's barn with it.*

What did the horse wear on her wedding day? *A Martinvale.*

How can you tell the winged horse loves her friends? *The way she pegagushes.*

How did the horse rescue its friend bad from the bad guys? *It went on a conquestrian.*

Why did the horse have a cellphone? *It was a mobile steed.*

How does a horse stay so stylish? *She follows mane-stream trends.*

How does a horse greet others?
"Howdy, gall-sup?"

Who do the police have in custody
for the murder of a winged horse?
Pegasuspects.

What kind of treats did the horse
request? *Hanovarious.*

What do funny horses drink at
parties? *Mock-tails.*

How did ponies send secret messages in World War 1? *Horse code.*

What kind of horse do you want to find in the produce aisle? *A fresh one.*

Why was the Clydesdale so rude? *It was coldblooded.*

What do winged horses eat for breakfast? *Egg-asus.*

How did the horse escape? *They forgot to close the gait.*

What does Pegasus say when he wins a bet? *You'll be o-wing me.*

What do hunter jumper horses eat for breakfast? *English muffins.*

Why was the male horse asked to leave? *It was smellding.*

What's a horses favorite stuffed animal? *A Kentucky furby.*

What do you call popcorn on a horse's back? *Corn on the cob.*

Why did the horse buck? *It was a rude-mare.*

Why did the horse bring its cup back to the water fountain? *It wanted a re-filly.*

What's a pony's favorite Shakespeare play? *The Taming of the Horseshrew.*

Where does a horse like to go to relax? *The breech.*

How did the horse get the teacher's attention? *"I have an equestion for you."*

Why did the horse need 8 wigs? *She was high mane-tenance.*

Why couldn't the winged horse stop and chat? *She was in a pegarush.*

How does a winged horse fill up its car? *With pe-gas-us.*

Why was the pony upset? *Her parents were getting a div-horse.*

Why did the horse leave her job? *There was high halternover.*

How did one horse break up with the other? *I'm so dun with you.*

Why did the horse name a river after itself? *It wanted an e-pony-m.*

Why didn't the horse's air conditioning work yet? *It hadn't been properly in-stallion-ed.*

What do you call a horse painting a buggy? *A horse-drawn carriage.*

Why did the horse get complimented at New York Fashion Week? *It had a great coat.*

What kind of horse can narrate a documentary? *The Morgan Freeman horse.*

What do you call a horse you can't find? *Horseback hiding.*

What's a horse's least favorite part of farming? *The crops.*

Why couldn't the horse get his money back? *It was non-refillyable.*

Why did the horse teach a class? *She is the master of her do-mane.*

What's a barreling horse's favorite movie genre? *Western.*

Why did they call the horse a baby?
It wouldn't stop cribbing.

How does a horse ask for something? *A requestrian.*

What is Superman's horse's only weakness? *Kryptoknight.*

Why didn't the horse like the dress?
It was too filly.

What do you call a horse doing a spin for a treat? *A carrotation.*

How do horses keep track of contacts? *In their addressage book.*

Who does a winged horse want to sell its product to? *The peg-masses.*

Why don't horses get sick? *They're good at pr-eventing.*

What's Pegasus' favorite playground toy? *The s-wing.*

How did the horse put up decorations? *It mounted them.*

How does a winged horse do its mane? *With a pegabrush.*

What did the horse wear on her wedding day? *Her favorite headpiece.*

Why didn't the horse say yes to the dress? *It didn't feel bridle enough.*

How could you tell the horse was getting sick? *It looked a little Clydes-pale.*

What does a horse drink on a night out? *An appletini.*

What's a wet horse called? *A water chestnut.*

Why didn't the horse speak out at the controversial event? *He thought better and bridled his tongue.*

What does a horse call an adventure? *An equest.*

Why did the horse put its hair on the wall? *It heard it needed another coat.*

What do you call two ponies playing? *Horsing around.*

Why did the horse stay at home so much? *Its house was made of applewood.*

Why was the horse giving out so many compliments? *It just used a soft brush.*

How does a horse make a sandwich? *With pure bread.*

How did the pony know he was going to get the promotion? *Her said he was a horse-shoe in.*

What type horse can you buy with one coin? *A quarter horse.*

What kind of horse would be on SNL? *A Will Ferrell horse.*

What kind of beer do horses drink? *Draft*.

What's a horse's favorite music festival? *Stagecoach*.

What do ponies put on hotdogs? *Horseradish*.

What kind of horse would Aladdin ride? *An Arabian.*

What do horses call surveys? *Equestionnaires*.

Who is a horse's favorite monster? *Flankenstein.*

How did the horse win money at the hockey game? *He bought a 50/50 snaffle ticket.*

Why was the horse allowed to leave the hospital? *It was determined stable.*

What weight class was the boxing horse in? *Feather weight.*

Why did the horse start speaking in an English accent? *It was using a Liverpool bit.*

What does the horse order at McDonald's? *Filly-o-Fish.*

Why would you bring a horse as a date? *They're good at dressage-ing up.*

Why did the horse think he was a king? *Everyone called him sire.*

What's a horse's favorite cottage activity? *Saddleboating.*

How do you get horses in the ocean? *Tell them there's a corral reef.*

Why doesn't the horse need a robe? *It has its own house-coat.*

What kind of car accident to horses often get into? *Rearing ends.*

Why was the horse so chill? *She was low mane-tenance.*

What kind of jewelry do horses like?
24 carrot gold.

What language do horses speak?
Canternese.

What do most horses get pulled over
for? *Busted taillights.*

Was the horse's tack too tight? *Just a
bit.*

How do Christian horses make
sandwiches? *Cross bread.*

What's an equestrian's favorite Taylor Swift song? *Whitehorse.*

How do horses get their future told? *Carrot readings.*

How could you tell the horse was generous? *She gave a lot to chariot-y.*

How does a horse make its decisions? *Spur of the moment.*

How do you know horses can run a marathon? *They can do cross country.*

What's a horse's best day ever? *Its hay-day.*

What do horses put in their protein shakes? *W-hay.*

How would a horse owner respond if you wanted to take their vet and farrier? *"You want distaff?"*

How do you make a horse look especially put together? *A dandy brush.*

How does a horse chase someone? *By tail-ing them.*

Why did the winged horse tell another he likes her? *He has a pegacrush.*

Why does the winged horse always look so embarrassed? *It's wearing pegablush.*

How could you tell the horse was well-travelled? *It was a global steed.*

What kind of cigarettes would a horse smoke? *Belmonts.*

What does a horse say when you ask if it wants to go for a run? *"Gall-yup."*

How does a horse reach for a treat? *It lunges.*

Where do horses go on vacation? *Flankfurt*.

Where do horses live in Harry Potter? *Diagonal Alley.*

How do winged horses walk if they become pirates? *Peg-asus legs.*

How did the pony get the bugs away? *It said, horse-shoo fly, don't bother me.*

What did the horse reply when asked if it would try water polo? *"I would dapple."*

What does a Clydesdale say when you offer them a carrot? *"Of course, my horse."*

What were the ponies most excited for in the meal? *The main horse.*

Where do most horses work for their first job? *Re-tail stores.*

What do horses use to eat?
Breastplates.

What type of car would a regular horse buy? *A Fjord Focus.*

Why was the pony so excited to be invited to a rally with the president? *It was a huge end-horse-ment.*

How does a horse drink wine? *With a de-canter.*

What did the teenage horse say when her phone broke? *I canter even.*

What does a horse do when it smells rotten seafood? *It scallops outta there.*

How could you tell the horse was getting old? *It was wither-ing away.*

How do ponies react when the opposing team comes on the field? *They horse-boo.*

What's happens to the sportiest horse? *It gets to be first horse-pick of the draft.*

Why did the horse climb Everest? *She liked mount-ains.*

What do you call old horses? *Ancient roans.*

How did the ponies stay in touch? *C-horse-pondence.*

Why couldn't the equestrian find the carrots? *They were down by the bay.*

What's a horse's favorite sport? *Saddleball.*

What do you call a rainbow you ride your horse on? *A rein-bow.*

Why didn't the horse tell her friend she was a thief? *She didn't want to saddle her with that information.*

Why does a horse's hair always look so good? *She mane-tains it.*

Why did the horse never get cold? *It was a Dutch warmblood.*

What do horses get after graduating university? *A pedegree.*

How does a horse get a suit fitted? *With a tail-or.*

How did the horse make payments? *In in-stallion-ments.*

What cartoon do horses like to watch? *Whinny the Pooh.*

What did the horse say to his friend that didn't come party last night? *You didn't turnout.*

What do you call a horse on a boat attached to land? *Docked.*

What does the winged horse do after it goes to the bathroom? *Pegaflushes.*

How does a horse tow its trailer? *With a Ford Bronco.*

What's does a winged horse like to munch on? *Pe-grass-us.*

What did the guard say to stop the horse from escaping? *Halt-her!*

Why did the horse go to jail? *The prosecutors failed to show the burden of hoof.*

What do you call a horse that leads the blind? *Horseback guiding.*

What kind of boy horses do girl horses want? *Studs.*

What's a horse's favorite bread? *Multi-grain.*

Why did the ponies get in trouble? *They kept foaling around.*

What's a horse's favorite snack? *Bits'n'Bites.*

What did the jockey respond when someone asked to ride his horse? *"Dis-mount is mine."*

Why did the horse like her new backpack? *The straps were adjustable.*

What's a horse's favorite grocery store? *No-fillies.*

How does a Pegasus ask her boyfriend to propose? *She says "You've got to put a wing on it."*

What did the pony say to the Jedi Knight before she left on her adventure? *"May the horse be with you."*

What do you call a pony running in a circle? *Centrifugal horse.*

What do winged horses attend in school? *Pegclasses.*

What does a horse call her best friend? *Her mane chick.*

How did the horse know the others were gossiping about him? *He herd.*

How do horses get to another star system? *They travel through intergalloptic space.*

What's a horse's favorite country singer? *Colt-on Underwood.*

What did one horse say to the other after he said he wanted to drop out? *That's an equestionable decision.*

What kind of car do fancy horses drive? *Mustangs.*

What do you call a horse running on a table? *A counter canter.*

Where do horses buy groceries? *Whinny-Dixie.*

What's the spiciest way to clean a horse? *With a curry comb.*

How did the horse break into the mainframe? *It was a hack.*

What did the horse reply when asked if it can jump 3 feet? *"I lope so!"*

Where do horses get their mane cut? *The hair-dressager.*

What would a winged horse play in a band? *The pegabass guitar.*

Why did they stop giving the horse grass? *They wanted it to be less green.*

What's a horse's favorite fruit?
Canterlope.

What do horses eat with their salad?
Dressage-ing.

Why do horses make good lawyers?
Attention to de-tail.

Where do horses go to the
bathroom? *The bathroom stall-ion.*

Why couldn't the baby horse eat
dessert? *It was foal.*

What is the lesser-known sport used to measure a horse's singing ability? *Carol racing.*

What would a winged horse put in the bathtub? *A pegaLush bath bomb.*

What's a horse's favorite animated movie? *Bolt.*

Why was the horse feeling a bit sick? *Its voice was a bit hoarse.*

Why are horses so good at the shooting range? *They're hunters.*

Why is Pegasus so smart? *He's all kno-wing.*

What did the ponies do when it was raining? *Stay ind-horse.*

Why was the horse sad she didn't get the job? *She was flanking on it.*

How do horses greet each other? *"Hayyyyy."*

What's a racehorse's favorite clothing brand? *Jockey*.

Who did the horse ask to be his second wife? *A manewer model.*

What does a winged horse drink from at a party? *A keg-asus.*

How do mares keep track of their boyfriends? *A stud book.*

What does a workhorse like to drink? *A Moscow Mule.*

What is the coldest type of horse? *A freezian.*

What's a horse's favorite makeup brand? *Neighhhbelline.*

Why does the horse go to school? *It brings her fulfillyment.*

Why couldn't the little girl ride the horse? *It was feeling bucky.*

What do you call a horse going down a waterslide? *Horseback sliding.*

What was the horse's best ballroom dance? *The Foxtrot.*

Why was Pegasus such a good ballerina? *He was flo-wing.*

What natural disaster took out the ancient horses? *A volcanic stirruption.*

What did the horse say when it saw a sheepdog? *"Why is your furlong?"*

How did the horse solve a murder? *Compiled newspaper clippings.*

Where do horses get their weaves from? *Mane.*

What do you say when your horse proposes to your other horse? *Call the marrier!*

What kind of horse would Bilbo Baggins ride? *A shire.*

Printed in Great Britain
by Amazon

61326004R00038